Crone's Book
of Magical Words

White as an eggshell,
White as a bone,
White as chalk

Or milk or the moon,
Is the written word
Of the ancient Crone,
Who works by wind,
Sun, water, and stone.

About the Author

Valerie Worth was a prolific writer whose work included numerous books of children's poetry and fiction for both young people and adults. In 1991, the National Council of Teachers of English honored her with their Poetry Award for Excellence in Poetry for Children. Her poems are vivid observations of the quiet rumblings of everyday objects. In all her writing, the careful attention to rhythm and sound and her striking images and metaphors make for engaging reading.

Valerie Worth was born in Philadelphia, and as a child she lived in Pennsylvania, Florida, and India. She attended Swarthmore College and graduated in 1955. Afterward, she settled in Clinton, New York, and continued her writing. She had many other interests, including astronomy, gardening, and meditation. Valerie Worth died in 1994. She is survived by her husband, George Bahlke, and three children.

Crone's Book of Magical Words

Valerie Worth

2000
Llewellyn Publications
St. Paul, Minnesota 55164-0383, U.S.A.

SECOND EDITION
Second printing, 2000
(Previously titled *The Crone's Book of Words*)
First edition published by Llewellyn Publications, 1971, twelve printings

Cover art and design: Lisa Novak and Anne Marie Garrison
Cover photo: Leo Tushaus
Interior design and editing: Kimberly Nightingale

Library of Congress Cataloging-in-Publication Data

Worth, Valerie.
    Crone's book of magical words / Valerie Worth.—2nd ed.
        p. cm.
Rev. ed. of: The crone's book of words.
ISBN: 1-56718-825-7
    1. Incantations. 2. Charms.   I. Worth, Valerie. Crone's book of words. II. Title.

GR540 .W65 1999
133.4'4—dc21   99-052699

The old-fashioned remedies in this book are historical references used for teaching purposes only. The recipes are not for commercial use or profit. The contents are not meant to diagnose, treat, prescribe, or substitute for consultation with a licensed healthcare professional.

Llewellyn Publications
A Division of Llewellyn Worldwide, Ltd.
P.O. Box 64383, Dept. K825-7
St. Paul, MN 55164-0383

Other Books by Valerie Worth

Small Poems, 1972
(Farrar, Straus & Giroux)

More Small Poems, 1976
(Farrar, Straus & Giroux)

Still More Small Poems, 1978
(Farrar, Straus & Giroux)

Curliques: The Fortunes of Two Pug Dogs, 1980
(Farrar, Straus & Giroux)

Gypsy Gold, 1983
(Farrar, Straus & Giroux)

Fox Hill, 1986
(Farrar, Straus & Giroux)

Small Poems Again, 1986
(Farrar, Straus & Giroux)

All the Small Poems, 1987
(Farrar, Straus & Giroux)

At Christmas Time, 1992
(Harper Collins)

All the Small Poems and Fourteen More, 1994
(Farrar, Straus & Giroux)

The Crone's Book of Charms & Spells, 1998
(Llewellyn Publications)

A Note from George Bahlke

Valerie Worth wrote these spells out of her great interest in the history of magic and her love of poetry. In rereading them, I have admired their powerful evocation of the spirit inherent in all occult wisdom. At the same time, readers should be aware that some of the charms, among them "To Afflict Another's Garden," "To Curse an Enemy," "To Decrease Another's Power," and "A Mirror Cipher for Revenge," are imitations of older magic; they were composed to be read, not practiced. Valerie would have been distressed if any of these charms were to bring harm to anyone; indeed, she thought poetry and magic should bring us joy and a sense of celebration, for her poetry itself was a ritual, a ritual she endeavored to express adequately and appropriately to the subject of the charm or poem she was working on.

Contents

Preface

Magic is the product of human intelligence; still dependent on this intelligence, it does not wither away. The old mysteries have only slightly changed, though humankind's regard for them and the means of dealing with them shift from age to age. The cosmos remains as significant and inscrutable as it ever was—birth, love, and death are no less poignant and inexorable; sorrow, pain, fear, joy, hope, and desire manifest themselves to the modern sensibilities essentially as they did to the primitive senses.

Today we are more in peril as a species than ever before; our ideas of salvation center on material and political remedy, while we are in awe of our works to the point that we must seek finally to limit them. These things are true to such a degree that we make a faith of reason; still, beneath the intellectual control that we assert run the same anarchies, the same primitive, or psychological, reactions to our environment that led first men to create irrational weapons for dealing with irrational phenomena. There have been only minor changes in these phenomena during the instant of human existence on our planet.

Religion has been an elaboration of such weapons, but religion now becomes more reasonable and less effective as it moves closer to the ethical and social problems of our society; stripped of its earlier magic, it abandons us psychologically. Looking to psychology itself, we find essentially the same meagerness, the same strictures upon the imagination. Hoping for a substitute in art, we meet again only a mirror of that rational culture that we have created but whose creations, ultimately, we are not. How, then, shall we confront our demons and our angels? How shall we express what we are, who are more than helpless but less than omnipotent?

It can only seem that we do insist on the unreasonable in the face of all reason; we do pursue, perhaps with laughter or with grimaces, but still pursue, impulses toward the stars of the astrologers, the candle burnings of the elder priests, the ancient magician's cryptic circles, and in such ways, the relationship between our own involuntary visions and that which is beyond mere routine as a solution to chaos.

This book arises from certain premises: that words themselves are a means to emotional control over exterior phenomena: that magic today is the same weapon that it was, even though we lay hands on it in a new spirit, even though we are uncertain of its uses and wield it unwittingly or even unwillingly; that all rituals, ancient and new, spring from the same vision of a possible order to life, an order that heals and reconciles effectively by its very roots in mental process. The rituals, or spells, or poems—and these names can all stand for the same thing—that are set down here deal with aspects of experience at once too simple and too complex for any other approach.

There is a traditional basis for many of these spells; there is a psychological basis for all of them. The past is so close to the present in this realm that it is unnecessary to distinguish between them, but possibilities for dealing with experience by appropriate verbal inventions are no fewer now, when drawn out of the newly convoluted psyche, than when they sprang from the primitive wrinkled brow. The rituals here, whether they are to be only imagined, or to be contemplated, or actually to be performed, are ultimately no more and no less than those of the ancients: rituals indeed, and therefore means of shaping reality according to the human will.

Whether they are effective or not is a matter of individual circumstance and discovery; but the human will is no petty toy, and the mind has already found itself in possession of forces that are beyond category and analysis. To attempt, through them, to control experience at all is at least to confront those forces and, perhaps, even, to draw upon them.

Cornwall, Vermont
1969

The Spirit

For Controlling the Senses

Draw the circle with red chalk,
Twice three feet from side to side;
Empower it, inscribe it thus:

Set beyond the outer edge
In five directions, each of these:
A lighted candle,
A ticking clock,
Incense burning,
A velvet mantle,
A goblet of wine.
Sprinkle within the double rim.

Drops of vinegar, grains of salt;
Enter the circle, wearing white,
Stand in the center, on the Sun;
Say these lines, with eyelids shut:

I am these five
Yet greater still;
I am as others
Yet unlike all;
While I spend
I am not consumed—
Let them come in
And be assumed,
But ever to serve,
Never to rule.

Gather the symbols from their places,
Set them upon the Planets' signs;
Treat them with honor, yet with strength:
Blow out the candle,
Pick up the clock,
Smother the incense,
Put on the mantle,
Drink the wine—
Step from the circle, walk from the room;
Do not return until next day's noon.

An Ablution for the New Year

New time demands new spirit; this purification is required: prepare a basin of snow, or of clear water iced, and scatter over it earth dried in the sun to a fine dust. The hands should then be immersed and chilled, the brow anointed and cooled, and these words said:

Substance wasted, substance spoiled, now be redeemed: seeing thyself in substance undefiled, forming thyself anew from this frail substance gathered and revived.

Thus should it be done at morning, and again at evening: to charge the original chaste intellect, the innocent purpose failed.

To Dispel Sorrow

When world and fate
Conspire to mark
Your life with lines
And characters dark,
Mold a tablet
Of earth or clay,
Write on it all
You would cast away—
All you regret,
All that you bear,
All that afflicts you,
All that you fear—
Break it and bury it
In the ground,
Saying this charm
To heal the wound:

Sorrow be dust
And dust dissolve:
Let all my grief
Go into this grave.

Against Enemies or Evil

Hang an ash bough
Over your door,
Fill your pockets
With iron nails,
Carry always
The mullein leaf,
But say these words
Against the worst:

I stand
In circles
Of light
That nothing
May cross.

To Escape Madness at the Full Moon

Follow these steps
To guard your wits
When the round Moon rises,
The gray Moon gazes,
The cold Moon crazes,
The mad Moon amazes:
Shroud all mirrors,
Curtain all windows,
Shut every door,
Cover your hair,
Wind red yarn
About your arm
And knot it thrice
While saying this:

LUNA LUSCA,
LUPA LURIDA,
LANA LIVIDA,
LAC LAPIDIA:
NON LATRO
SED LATEO.

A Magical Inscription for Endurance

To stand like granite,
Stout as the planet,
Mark on a rock
With a stick of chalk:

Though chalk is frail
And cannot prevail,
You shall be firm
As crystal or stone.

A Sage Tea for the Mind

The gray-leaved sage
Stands fresh and fine
When even trees
Fall prey to time;
Pluck its growth,
Brew an infusion
Against all darkness
And confusion;
Drink its strength,
With these words:

Sage make green
The winter rain:
Charm the demon
From my brain.

To Become Invisible

Fern seed
In your pocket
Will hide you
From some,
But to be free
Of everyone,
You must go away
Where water lies
Quiet, and look
To find your face—
Then scatter
The seeds across
Your image
Until
It departs.

To Embrace Solitude

Go into your house
And fasten the windows,
Block the chimneys,
Lock the doors;
Stop up the keyholes,
Draw the curtains,
Say these words
To all betrayers:

I am my own today,
Nor any other shall steal me away.

Drink to your strength
A glass of wine,
Then sit three hours
In silence, alone,
Before you go forth again.

To Avert Temptation

If the demon approaches
And gently beseeches
Your custom and favor,
And offers you silver
Or gold for your weakness,
Or feasts of great sweetness,
Or beauty past wasting,
Or love everlasting,
Or pleasures unending,
To buy your unbending,
Cut from a tangle
Of thorns a long bramble,
Twist it around
To a ring on the ground,
Pretend you would enter,
Then spit in its center,
And turn back his harm
By repeating this charm:

DUMUS DIABOLO!
ILLIGO ILLICO!

To Reject the Evil Self

The guilt that rests upon your head,
The evil stain upon your hand,
May be removed: go forth and cast
Your shadow dark upon the land—
Pierce the image with a stake
And drive it with a heavy stone;
Let both weapons stay to mark
The deed you shed, the self you scorn.

For an Absolution

In a shaded room
Burn candles three
Whose wax is black
As ebony;
Let incense cloud
And thicken the air,
Then write these words
Against despair:

DOLOR FUMOSUS
ANIMUS ATRATUS
IN LUCTU SUM
SIGNO SIGNUM

Burn the paper
And powder its ash
In a shallow bowl
Of polished brass;
Cover your hands
With this dark dust—
Your past will be cleansed,
Your future blessed.

To Be Rid of Anger

If the house is infected by a rage that will not be appeased, whether yours or another's, you must find a toad in the garden and shut him up in a wicker basket. Take this to where the afflicted sleeps and set it beneath his bed, letting it remain there through a whole night. In the morning draw the basket out, bear it to a cross-roads, and release the toad with these words:

Hence, toad,
Take thy road,
Get thee gone
And all thy bane;
Carry this anger
To a stranger,
Bring it never
Home again.

To Sweeten Another's Disposition

Thus turn his scorn to kindest love:
Steal from him the left-hand glove;
With shining sugar fill it full
And tie it, that it may not spill,
With satin ribbons, blue and green;
Then, when the deed may pass unseen,
Hide it underneath his pillow—
He shall sleep, and melt, and mellow.

To Enchant an Apple

Pick your apple
When the Moon
Has waned three days;
Breathe upon
Its green cheek,
Rub it with
A scarlet cloth,
Saying:

Fire sweet
And fire red,
Warm the heart
And turn the head

Kiss the red half,
Put it later
In another's hand—
Who holds it
Shall weaken,
Who eats it
Shall be yours.

A Love Potion

For a potion to excite another's affections, take a gill of
good red wine and add to it these: a teaspoonful each of
rosemary leaves, of anise seed, of cloves, of clear honey,
and of orange rind, with a pinch of ground cumin and
three green leaves from the rose geranium. Mix them in
a saucepan over the fire and bring all to boiling, then
gently stir and simmer them while you slowly count to
one hundred. Remove the pan to a cool place until its
contents cease to steam; then strain them through a
fine sieve, and return the liquid to heat again upon the
fire. When sweet vapors rise, pour the potion into a
cup and deliver it to the one whose love you would
sweeten and warm; it shall not fail, unless performed by
one whose heart and household keep slatternly habits.

To Win Another's Love

Open a bird that is soon to be roasted,
Draw from its body the shining heart,
Let it with drops of blood be basted,
Seethe it in wine and set it apart;
When it is cool, in your left hand take it;
Squeezing it tight as your fingers can,
Say these words to warm it and wake it,
So to possess any maiden or man:

My fire is thine,
Thy blood my wine:
Thy love, my dove,
Must soon be mine.

Halve, with the blade of a silver knife,
Its yielding flesh, delicious and sweet,
Then taste it, munch it, swallow its life—
Next to your own that heart shall beat.

A Fire Spell for Love

Take twelve candles, white and tall,
Dress them with sweet-scented oil,
Set them on a table spread
With velvet cloth of ruby red
To form a figure of three sides;
Light their wicks, then say these words:

Fire, spirit of the Sun,
Wax, thou melting flesh of Earth,
Prove this work that I have done,
Bring me love, and beggar death:
Let me be myself consumed
Not by darkness but by light,
Warmth, not cold, until I spend
My final flame against the night.

Watch the candles downward burn,
In their sockets let them drown;
Give the wick-ends to that one
Whose love must be your Earth and Sun.

To Enchant a Ring for Marrying

Buy a ring of common metal,
Plain and narrow, colored gold,
To fit the wedding finger well;
Drop it in a vessel filled
Half with wine and half with water,
Add one oak leaf, one of willow,
Two of bay and two of grass,
And the name of whom you love
Written on a silver paper;
Keep the vessel covered tight
Near a window, in the sun,
From crescent Moon until the full—
Then rub the ring and wear it hidden
On a string around your neck;
But never tell the name you seek
Until you take it for your own.

A Charm to Send in the Name of Love

Fold a white paper
In half three times,
On one of the squares
Inscribe this rhyme,
In ink like blood
Or crimson wine:

Drawn from my hand
These words run blood
Or wine, not ink,
Thy lip to woo:
So may they spend
My heart's sweet flood,
Bidding thee drink
The love I brew.

Kiss it, address it,
And send it away,
But keep your name secret
A year and a day.

To Recall One Who Is Unfaithful

Who turns from you shall yet be bound
If signs of him may still be found
Within your house—one hair or thread,
Fragment or color, scent or word,
Or any thing that bears his touch—
This spell turns little into much:
Seal the relic in a box
With seven strings tied round for locks,
Each one tight-knotted seven times:
Then set on it these seven signs:

$$V A K \infty X \Omega \mathsf{\gamma}$$

Hide it in darkness, out of sight,
Until the next Moon's seventh night,
Then send it to the one you seek—
He must return within a week.

To Favor a Marriage

Let two who are wed
Go into an open meadow
Before the grass is harvested:
Each must gather
As much of the living hay
As his own left hand can hold;
Then in the field they shall stay
And weave of the stalks two figures—
The woman shall fashion a woman,
And the man shall fashion a man,
And together these shall be wound
With a golden stem of grass,
Around and around
And knotted at last.
Then they shall set these images
Deep in the ground,
To be bedded and covered with earth,
Hidden by grass that is growing still;
And the couple shall stand
Facing each other and say:

We are grown and gathered and bound
And the binding is well;
We are fixed at the hip and the hand
And the head and the heel;

We are planted beneath the land,
Forever to wheel
As the Earth and the Sun are wound
On a golden reel,
As the ripening grasses stand
And pale and fall.

For Looking into Mirrors

Look to the left,
Look to the right,
Look in the glass
And say these lines:

Quicksilver
Mirror silver
Show me
My true face.

Look at the eyes:
If their black centers
Be shrunk and small,
The mirror lies.

To Be Said When Passing a Cemetery

Knit your fingers,
Hold your breath,
Say to yourself
This verse for death:

Keeper of bones
I know thy face,
But I shall yet
Outstrip thy pace.

To Spin Thread into Words (an Exercise in Mourning)

Fasten the lock,
Stop the clock,
Sit alone
In a silent room;
Speak aloud
To fashion a shroud
And warm the dead
With words of THREAD:

HEAR THE HART
TREAD THE EARTH,
HEAR THE DART
EAT THE HERD,
HEAR THE RAT
TEAR THE HEAD—
AH DEAR HEART,
DARE DEATH!

To Write a Letter to the Beloved Dead

In this manner the letter must be written: first, the ink prepared from soot mixed with pale wine; next, the pen made, shaped from a quill never before cut; then, the paper arranged on a table between two black candles. At the top of the paper this inscription should be set:

See now, thou who are mourned, the nature of this mourning: as thou knowest even now my sorrow, so on this paper do I doubly affirm it. I write thee my heart here, for thy sight and mine only—that we may be bound by such silent words even better than when our words were spoken. Receive, then, this document as sign and token of my commitment: not to forget thee, nor to cease mourning for thee, until my own life shall be ended.

Write down then the essence of your grief, the substance of your devotion, and such aspects of memory as you would fix forever. When this has been accomplished, fold the paper thrice and seal it, along with sweet herbs, in a small box which should then be buried in the ground, or burned in a fire of fragrant wood. The letter shall thus be received.

The World

To Be Safe from Fires

In wet woods by water
Find the shy salamander,
Catch him in a cage of willows woven,
Bring him home in haste,
Set him down beside the hearth
While four sallow sticks, crossed, shall burn;
Then cast water from a pitcher upon them,
And when they are dead
Say this, to bind the protection:

Salamander, salamander
Turn fire to water
Under this house
And over this house.

Carry his cage through every room,
Then let him out and set him free
Among the lowest foundation stones standing,
There to hide and be safe
And keep you well forever.

To Protect a Garden from Pests . . .

Mix in a vessel of rusted iron
Oils of camphor and wintergreen,
Oil of spearmint, oil of clove,
A spoonful of blood and a glass of wine;
Pour them about the threatened ground;
Then mark in red on a flag of white
This charge, that puts all foes to flight:

NEPENTHE NEPENTHE
DISTINE DEFENDE

Fix this banner upon a pole
Driven deep in the garden soil—
Thus it will banish beast or fowl.

and Against Weeds in the Garden

Under a Waning Moon, break one leaf from the garden's tallest weed; crush it with your teeth, spit the fragments out upon the earth, and say,

MALUM DESPUO
HOSTEM VENENO
CAEDO CAEDO

Cut the stalk off short with a silver knife; spread a handful of salt above the hidden root. All the garden bears witness to this curse, and its enemies must soon withdraw.

To Afflict Another's Garden

That garden so swollen
With prizes and pride
May find its wealth stolen,
Its boasting belied:
There, from your own,
Send failure and blight
By anointing a stone
With a paste of these eight—
The aphid, the snail,
The slug and the beetle,
The rust and the gall,
The mildew, the spittle—
All smashed in a mortar
And stirred to a slime,
Then dried into a powder
And moistened with brine.
Hold hidden the curse
In your hand when you call
Then think of this verse
While you let the stone fall:

Proud flowers here
Grow sick and sere;
Foul pests descend,
This Eden end.

To Send Away Mice and Rats

Where the rat or mouse
Has insulted your house
With scrabbling paw
And ruinous jaw,
You must sprinkle with blood
The path he has trod,
Then mark on his walk
These words, in chalk:

MUS, MUS,
MONEO:
MUNIO
MORDEO
MUTILO.

So threaten his life
And bring him to grief.

To Treat a Leaking House

If humid stain
Of snow or rain
On ceiling or wall
Lets swell and fall
The watery drop,
Catch in a cup
That sorry brew,
Set it to stew
Beside the fire
With garnish dire:
Dead fly,
Potato eye,
Hair long,
Mustard strong,
Milk sour,
Dusty flour.
Stir to a paste
This evil waste,
Carry it there,
The flaw to dare,
Saying these lines:

Now heal, and let
Thy weakness wane,
Let water seek
Its proper drain.
Or take this plaster
For thy pain.

If it remains,
Smother the spot
With a poultice thick—
Then leave it there
For all of an hour.

Against the Domestic Demons

All treasures that in your house are found
Are only demons that dance you round;
Their shapes like plates and lamps and chairs
Snatch at your brain and catch it in snares;
If you would loose the talons that tease,
And live by spirits more worthy than these,
Write upon leather, ancient and brown,
The names of all that grapple you down—
The Meissen plates, the lamp of Towle,
The Sheraton chairs, the Sevres bowl,
The carpet, the curtains, the papered wall,
The spoons and the goblets—goblins all,
And countless others that take their pleasure
Drinking your soul for their daily measure;
Cast their names in a raging fire;
Say these words, your strength to inspire:

Who winds me about
Go out, go out!
When I turn round
I soon shall find
Mere dust and ash,
Poor trappings and trash,
All rigid and dead,
Their powers fled.

An Inscription to Be Written on a Windowpane . . .

Darkness lies
Where it is born,
But Sun flies
To light this room.

and over a Doorway

Who comes to me I keep,
Who goes from me I free
Yet against all I stand
Who carry not my key.

For Reading a Magical Word Square

Write these words on paper:

TREE
ROAD
EAVE
EDEN

Read from west to east
And north to south,
Then speak aloud:

TREE of knowledge,
ROAD of pain,
EAVE of home,
EDEN again.

If you solve this riddle
Burn the paper on your hearth:
It will keep the house
From sorrow, all year long.

For Pleasing the Household Spirits

From a golden broom pluck five long straws,
Light them as tapers at the fire;
Carry them through the house, and cause
Their subtle smoke to thicken the air—
Then summon good fortune with this spell:

Wraiths of the house,
Take heart and live:
To every chamber
This light I give,
To every corner
This breath I send—
Approve and favor
My willing hand

If you would please them doubly well,
Sprinkle the floor with leaves of tea
And orris powder and grains of salt—
Then sweep with the broom, until you free
Each crack and crevice from speck or fault.

For Rejecting Fine Clothing

Put on garments never worn,
Spread on the floor a sheet untorn,
Stand in its center, light a match:
While it burns, be still and watch,
Then blow it out and scorn its fate,
Putting all vanity to flight:

The flame is gone,
Its life is flown;
Nothing remains
But ash and bone:
If noble coverings
Share my dust,
Why shall I love
What must be lost?
Lust of the loom
Go forth, begone!
I stand, I burn,
I wear the Sun!

Rend your clothing, rip the sheet,
Tread them beneath your naked feet;
Bathe anew, and wear thereafter
Weeds befitting your mortal fever.

To Keep Beauty from Fading

When all your face appears most fair,
When comets and meteors gild your hair,
And in your eyes the Moon and sun
Contest, surrender, and burn as one,
When ivory Venus smoothes your brow,
And Mars recurves your lips' red bow,
Make haste to utter this binding verse
And hold the stars on their kindest course:

Figures of fire
That shift and change,
Planets that move
By heaven's hinge,
Be signed and fixed
Forever here,
And close my image
Within thy sphere.

Measure a yard of golden string,
Loose from your fingers let it swing,
Then tie it in thirteen sturdy knots—
Hide it among your scents and pots.

To Turn the Hair Long and Golden

To spin brown straw,
Black weeds, red hay,
Into a stream
Of golden threads
That wind from the head
Like enchanted waters,
Rushing in torrents
Over the shoulders,
Curling to flowers
About the feet:
Gather from meadows
Still unmown
All yellow bloom
That fits the season—
Goat's-beard, mustard,
Goldenrod, trefoil,
Buttercup, dandelion,
King Devil, cinquefoil.
Chop them fine
And crush them down
Within a cauldron,
Boil in seven
Quarts of rain
From noon to sunset;
Cool and strain
Then rinse the hair
For seven days
In this gold wine.

To Keep the Hair from Falling

At sunrise, measure a spoonful each
And mix in a saucepan all of these:
Thread of saffron,
Anise seed,
Root of ginger,
Apple wine,
Clover nectar,
Cinnamon bark,
Oil of olives,
Leaves of pine.
Stir them, simmer them, saying this:

Spirits, conjure
Phoenix flowers
From the ashes
Of the dead:
Tell each hair
That touches thee
To hold forever
To my head

Strain them into a gill of milk
Mixed with an ounce of melted soap:
Warm the whole until it foams,
Then wash the hair, and nourish hope.

A Potion for Youth Preserved

These four, one spoonful each, combine:
Juice of apples freshly pressed,
Cider aged past seven days,
Apple vinegar, tart and brown,
Apple brandy, clear and strong;
Add to these an ounce of honey,
One scant drop of wintergreen;
Stir them, warm them, mix them well,
And take the tonic every dawn,
Saying this to work the spell:

If I must pay
The apple's price,
I shall be young
As well as wise,
Filling my cup
With honeyed days
And hours as green
As Eden's grass.

A Pact with a Tree for Longevity

Seek the darkness of a wood
Where oak and elm and maple brood,
Kneel before the greatest tree
That stands among that company,
Bury near its roots profound
A penny in the yielding ground,
Rise, and trace upon its bark
This verse, the covenant to mark:

Ancient tree
I offer thee
This mortal coin
As gift and sign:
Guard my fate
Both soon and late,
And let my rust
Grow green at last.

Seal the burial with a stone;
Leave it, and do not return
Until one lunar month has passed,
Then go and part the fertile dust—
If the coin has changed to green,
The forest's years shall be your own.

For Beauty after Death

Fungus, worm,
And fat corruption
Feed on the unwary;
But for a fair corpse,
There is this potpourri:

Wrap the body
In black velvet,
Sew it tight
With silver thread,
Bind it round
With three gold ribbons,
Kiss its foot
And heart and head,
In the coffin
Scatter broken
Roots of flag
And roots of culver,
Ambergris
And civet musk,
And the leaves
Of sweet-clover:
Pack the box
With petals, then,
Fallen from

The damask rose—
But do not open
It again,
When at last
The lid you close.

A Moon Vow for the Loss of Weight

When the Moon shows cold and slender,
    Stand beneath her starved light,
    Wearing only white and silver—
        Say, to whet her appetite,

      I make my vow to fast until
    This crescent Moon shines round and full;
      While she waxes let me wane:
      I must lose, that she may gain.

    While she grows, take silver wine,
        Silver water, silver milk,
    And bread like snow or linen fine,
      And fish as clear as ice or silk—
      But only these, and less of all
Than you would wish, to feed her well.

For the Art of Cookery

Tie up a bunch of these good herbs,
Basil, savory, mint, and dill;
Drench them in water drawn from the tap,
And sprinkle the kitchen—lintel and sill,
Shelf and canister, table and stove,
Cupboard and wall and window and floor,
Crockery, cutlery, napery, all—
With drops from the stalks, delicious and pure;
Then crush the bouquet in both your hands,
Breathe its scent, and whisper this spell:

Sweeten the oven,
Sweeten the pot,
Sweeten the cold
And sweeten the hot—
Summon thy virtues
Into this place
To teach me patience
And skill and grace.

Make from the leaves a strengthening tea,
Drink it, and keep your kitchen well.

To Defeat the Demon Tobacco

Grasp the poison-breathing weed,
Give him fire for his greed,
Taste his sweet and cruel savor,
Smiling, praise his deadly favor;
Then when he suspects you least,
Quick deceive the subtle beast—
Break his back and crush to death
His fawning image on your hearth;
Say these words (and say them ever
When his downfall you would conjure):

HERBA MALEFICA
ADURO
ADEDO
ADIMO

Against an Excess of Drink

Before those serpent alcohols
That tempt the tongue and soothe the brain
Shall rise and wind their glittering coils
About your feverish fears again,
Treat them firmly, do not fail
Before their clear hypnotic eyes;
Confess their power, yet prevail
Before they learn to turn and tease:
Utter this charm, that wit and will
May stare them down and hold them still:

Knowledge I have
While thou hast none,
I can make songs
Beyond thy tongue;
All of thy offerings
First were mine:
I keep my spirit
And need not thine.

Then raise to your lips a glass of wine—
Spit in it, empty it down the drain.

To Dispel Slander

When you are free
From any deed
Deserving blame,
Whoever speaks
An evil word
Against your name
Must be rebuked—
And all your works
Restored to fame:
A length of string
In melted wax
Must soon be laid,
Hung up to dry,
And now in inks
Of black and red
Be dipped and raised—
Thus drop by drop
Its stains to shed.
Meanwhile, let this verse be said:

Blood and rot,
Blight and spot,
Touch me not:
Run to spill
Over all
Who wish me ill.

A Hollyhock Spell for Riches

The hollyhock blooms in summer,
Its seeds in autumn fall:
Then, in a folded paper,
Save them, gather them all—
The loose seeds,
The brown seeds,
The dry seeds,
The round seeds,
The seeds like tarnished pennies
That pay for the blossoms tall;
Bury their rusty treasure
Next to a southern wall—
With a mint coin,
An ancient coin,
A silver coin,
A copper coin:
By spring your wealth shall measure
Twelve times this sowing small.

For Success on an Important Occasion

Steep in a bath
A bowlful of leaves
From three or four
Or five of these:
Marigold, celery,
Mint and grass,
Nasturtium, parsley,
Fennel and cress.
When the brew is green
And the steam is sweet,
Lie in the water
And thrice repeat:

I shall bathe
And I shall be
As green and strong,
Good herbs, as thee;
Draw me favor,
Draw me fame,
Draw bright honor
To my name.

Rise from the water
Thrice empowered;
Wear those virtues
You have conjured.

To Obtain a Particular
Appointment or Position

When night has fallen fully,
Raise one candle's fire
And write on virgin paper
All that you desire;
If any man can aid you,
There inscribe his name,
Followed by these others
For power, skill, and fame:

HELIMAZ

FERIDOX

SOLADAR

Brush every word thereon
With a ragged crust of bread;
Then shred the paper, soak it
In water tinted red;
Wring it, press it small
As a lump of sodden dough—
Fling it from the house
As far as it will go.

For the Efficacy of an Important Letter

When the letter has been sealed,
Set it on a table
Newly covered with a cloth
As black as ink or sable;
Pour around it clean salt
To form a silver circle;
Recite this verse of power
To render it most subtle:

> *Words that run*
> *Before my pace*
> *And carry me*
> *Beyond this place,*
> *Please the eyes*
> *That greet thee next,*
> *And work my will*
> *Within thy text.*

Fold the cloth to cover it,
And kiss the folds; release it
Soon to start upon its course,
Lest jealous hands should seize it.

Before Flight

You who would dare
To journey by air
Must first be freed
From folly and pride:
In sunlight stand
And pass your hand
Near to the gleam
Of a candle's flame;
Kindle a feather
Within its fire,
And when it is black,
Smother the wick;
Gather soft wax
And fill the cracks
Under your nails—
Then say this spell:

Too near to the Sun
I may not fly,
Scorched I should run
From his mocking eye—
Yet far from his scorn,
Below his sway,
Let me be borne
And spared this day.

To Be Said When Crossing a Bridge

In air but not flying,
Nor on the earth walking,
Nor in a boat riding,
Still cross without doubting—
The way will uphold you
If you will say boldly:

Bridge, be strong
From end to end,
And let me pass
From land to land.

For a Safe Return

In a small bag
Of supple leather
Or brown cloth,
Assemble these:

A stone the size
Of a pigeon's egg,
A spoonful of ash
From the morning hearth,
A chip of bark
From the tallest tree,
A pinch of earth,
A curl of dust,
A blade of grass,

All gathered from
The place you leave;
Add a lodestone
Or small magnet,
Tie the bag
With a strip of vine;
Wear it around
Your neck, on a thong—
Then do not grieve,
You must return.

When Taking Up Residence in a New Place

Sweeten the threshold on that day
When first you enter the house to stay;
Anoint the step in front of the door
With fixatives, balms, and oils rare:
Combine a drop or a grain of each—
Castoreum, civet, and ambergris,
Benzoin, storax, and orris root,
Lemonwood, sandalwood, bergamot,
Geranium, lavender, myrrh, and mace,
Or other pure essence to please your taste—
Then add grain spirits, pure and fair,
Stir with a brush of camel's hair,
And paint this sign where your foot must tread:

Walk there, and let the house be glad.

For an Improved State of Health

Fold in a scrap
Of velvet cloth
These treasures six
To bring you health:
Leaves of tea,
Flowers of lavender,
Ginger and salt
And clove and camphor;
Tie up the charm
With a scarlet thread,
Keep it beside
Your nightly bed;
Breathe it on waking
Every day—
You must be healed,
And healed must stay.

A Cider Potion for Strength

If cider is pressed
When the apples are warm,
Its russet taste
Must turn you strong;
Heat it with cloves,
With cinnamon long,
Drink it soon
And read this song:

Apple rust
And cinnamon rust
And cloves like rusty nails,
Turn my skull
To an iron wall,
My ribs to iron rails.

For an Elixir of Honey

When the day approaches noon,
Hold up honey to the sun,
That their double gold may run
Shining together, mixed as one.
Drink three spoonfuls,
Then say this:

Sun charge me,
Gold serve me,
Alchemy change me,
Honey preserve me.

A Horseshoe Charm for the Headache

This iron crescent,
Brown and old,
Is worth as much
As virgin gold;
Grasp both ends,
The center hold
Hard to your brow,
Heavy and cold;
Let this healing
Verse be told:

Good metal loosed
From horse's hoof,
Draw from my brain
These nails of pain:
Cast them away,
Rust them away,
Keep them away.

To Overcome Insomnia

To catch and keep
Fleet-footed sleep,
You must prepare
A subtle snare:
Lie as if dead
Upon your bed,
Stilling his fear,
Luring him near,
Then say this charm
To bind him firm:

MORPHEUS
SOPOR
SOMNIFICUS
SOMNIFER

If, even so,
He would turn and go,
Repeat this spell
Until he is still:

TOLIXA
OLIXAT
LIXATO
IXATOL
XATOLI
ATOLIX

Against Evil Dreams

The nightmare will toss
Its cold black mane
And gallop on ebony hoofs
From your pillow, away
As far as the Moon, if you say:

Thou evil thing
Of darkness born,
Of tail and wing
And snout and horn,
Fly from me
From now till morn.

Then think of the fire
That burns by day:
Sun in his glistening chariot,
Drawn by foam-white
Stallions, out of the sea.

To Guard Against Poisoned Food or Drink

To render pure
The plate or cup,
Do this before
You dare to sup:
Hold a walnut
Against your mouth,
Set it down
Upon the hearth,
Crack its shell
Beneath an axe,
Striking six times
With these words six:

NUX
HEX
NEX
TUX
TAX
PAX

Cast its fragments
Into the fire—
They shall burn,
Your ills to bear,
Your fate to turn,
Your life to spare.

Against Poison Ivy

Those ivy leaves
With demon tongues
That lick the hand
To blister it,
May yet be tamed
And set at naught
By those who will
By this be taught:
Learn the spot
Where jewelweed
Or touch-me-not
Or orange balsam—
One, by three
Names known—
Is grown;
Pluck the plants
Close to the roots,
Crush them, spread
The juices where
Corruption lies
Upon the skin,
Or might lie soon,
And say this rhyme:

Jewelweed
Starve ivy's greed,
Touch-me-not
Stay ivy's rot,
Orange balsam
Stop ivy's poison.

Cover the place
With further leaves
And bind them on;
The evil touch
Will soon be gone.

To Cure a Wart

Stamp within a silver cup
Mullein and houseleek together
Stir them with a sparrow's feather,
Let it draw the juices up;
Twenty times upon one day,
Brush them over the excrescence;
Under sunlight dry the essence—
Soon the wart must shrink away.

A Fertility Charm

On an egg whose shell
Is brown or pink,
Sign these signs
In grass-green ink:

☼ ♂ ⊕ ♀ ⛤

Bury it deep
In an earth-filled pot,
Let this stand
Where the sun is hot;
Sow on its surface
Seeds of grass,
Water them well
While nine weeks pass;
Gather the crop,
Bind it with thread,
Let it hang always
Above your bed.

For Obtaining a Male Child

Now thus invoke the striding Sun
To touch the infant in the womb
And give him flesh of manly flame—
Gold limb, gold beard, gold seed, gold name:
On paper mark this secret sign,

Then tie it, scrolled, with golden twine,
And cast it in the fire's mouth—
That it may rise, a shining breath,
To call its words across the sky
Where Sun's paternal powers lie.

For a Female Child

To form a daughter in the womb,
Trace this figure at New Moon,
On silver foil, with a silver spoon:

Crush the foil to make a sphere,
Cast it into waters near,
Whisper in the Moon's white ear:

O Maiden, feed
This silver seed,
In water's lap,
By water's pap,
Until its phase
Grows round with days—
That I may see
A child like thee.

For Naming the Unborn

When the womb is six months full,
Carry wine in a silver bowl
To a place where sun may turn it gold;
There, on a dozen chips of wood,
Write twelve names to name the child—
Male and female, six of each;
Let them drift upon the flood,
While, with eyes closed, forth you reach
And choose the name that meets your hand:
Draw the fragment out, and stand
Facing the sun, to read its sign
Inscribed forever from this time;
Now draw others, until you find
The other sex, to match its twin—
And know that either name is good,
So given by sun and wine and wood.

To Use the Herb Motherwort for an Easy Travail

When motherwort, undaunted weed,
Has sprung and flowered and gone to seed,
Gather the stalks with heads and leaves,
Tie them in cords to five strong sheaves;
Batter their tips against a wall
Until the seeds, sharp-spined, shall fall,
And when they are scattered upon the ground,
These words will render the womb unbound:

Seeds that wound,
Husks that bind,
Leave only peace
And joy behind:
Take away pain,
Let strength remain.

Untie the stalks and strip them bare,
Fold their leaves in a velvet square,
Sew up the charm with yellow thread:
As soon as the woman is brought to bed,
See that she hold it in her hand
For ease, as weeds are born from the land.

The Conjuror

To Curse an Enemy

In the dark of the Moon, spread a table with some coarse cloth of dark color, ragged and foul with dust. At the four corners set black candles unlit, and in the table's center an open box made of wood. Now on a small, flat stone inscribe his name, written reversed, whose life you would shadow and starve; spit upon it, set it within the box; then light the four candles with a burning straw or taper. When all is so prepared, cast into the box a handful of bitter weeds, chicory, dandelion, or others, and fix the curse with these words:

That thou shalt be turned into a stone,
And that all thy wits shall be turned front to back,
And that over thy face the loathsomeness shall creep,
And that as in a coffin thy limbs shall be bound,
And that light shall be withheld from thine eyes,
And that thy house and lands shall be impoverished
and spoiled,
And that all nourishment shall taste to thy tongue as
wormwood,
And that thou shalt be held alien from thy fellow man
And that these things shall be so until I release thee,
I spread this table and mark this stone
And spit upon it and conceal it,

And light these candles and apply these poisons,
And fix this curse upon thee
In the names of the four fires
Whose names are RIL, YUT, SAR, and LOD,
Who shall consume thee as they are consumed.

Remain watching by the candles until they are burnt out. Then these things may be taken away, but the stone must be buried near your house until the curse is withdrawn.

To Employ the Spirits of Darkness

To yoke the demons of the night,
Cut a fork of sapling oak,
Strip its bark and shake the wand
To and fro across the dark—
Send them ranging through the land
To do your will, by this command:

LAMIAE
LARVAE
LEMURES
PASSIM, PASSIM!

To Control a Malefactor

Take his name
And mince it fine,
Weave from his vigor
A subtle figure,
Spell him down,
Across and around:

MALEFA
ALEFAC
LEFACT
EFACTO
FACTOR

He may not breathe
Without your leave.

To Decrease Another's Power

To shrink his lust
And wither his dust,
Call the first,
Diminish the rest,
Whisper the last:

NORODAROGOR
RODAROGOR
DAROGOR
ROGOR
OGOR
OR

To Increase One's Own Power

Lie down as dead,
Then upward waken;
Raise this word
Your strength to quicken:

ON
ORON
DORON
RADORON
GORODORON
ROGORODORON

A Figure for Influence over Another

If with fetters
You would tame
The angry foe,
Or bind with shame
The faithless friend,
Draw this figure
In red ink:

In the corners
That remain
Mark four letters
Of his name;
Burn the paper;
Say this charm:

Circle him round,
Cross him within,
Turn him about,
And cast him out.

A Mirror Cipher for Revenge

An evil self
May lie within
The mirror's smooth
And silver skin;
Let your darkest
Work be done
By hands that hide
From sight and sun:
Make of wax
An image small
To bind the man
Who serves you ill,
Cast it in
A boiling pot,
Then print these letters
Close and neat
Upon a paper:

YOTYM MIHWYM
XAWYHT XIMI
TAVTOH YMTAHT
XATYAM TIWYHT

Hold it straight
Before the glass
To see his plight
(Your hands reversed
Will work his fate.)

For Breaking a Curse

Gather certain fallen twigs:
One of hazel, one of oak,
One of elm, and one of willow;
Hold them to the fire's smoke,
Say this softly, seven times all:

Turner be turned,
Burner be burned:
Let only good
Come out of this wood.

Spit on each and break it small
Cast them in the fire's mouth—
The curse will die with the fire's death.

In Summoning a Ghost

For conversation
With the dead,
Attend to ceremony;
Avoid the grave's
Annoyance, speaking
Always gently:

Earth, bone,
And winding sheet,
Let this spirit
Come to me—
Yet send it
In peace,
Or not at all.

If it come,
It should be offered
White wine,
Not red;
And knelt to,
From pity.

To Raise the Dead for a Prophecy

In a circle of string
With twelve knots fine
On a center of stone
With a wand of bone,
Knock at the earth
And summon him forth:

Spirit, we call
From Death's sweet thrall
Thy barren rib
And wasted lip—
Pity our life
And bring us truth.

To Free a House from Haunting

The Presence that stands
Upon the stairs,
The unseen hands
That move the chairs,
The lights that play
Across the wall,
The stains that stay,
The plates that fall,
The mist, the chill,
The wandering scents—
This gentle spell
Must speed them hence:
At midnight, set
A table neat,
With cup and plate
And wine and meat;
Invite the ghost
To sit and feast,
As any host
Should urge a guest;
Presently, clear
The meal away,
Then open the door
And softly say:

Quick or dead,
Thou art fed:
Cease to grieve,
And take thy leave.

Bid him depart—
But should he remain,
Be calm, take heart,
And feast him again.

For All-Hallow's Eve

When the white dog is out
And trots all about
Under the clouds
That are over the Moon,
And the hag with her broom
Rides high on the wind,
And the cat on the fence
Spits even at friends,
Then it is right
To conjure a light
Against every spirit
That shadows the night.
Thus say:

Let the pumpkin's
Candle glare
Into darkness
Everywhere;
Burn all evil
From the air!

When it is dark
And the black trees roar,
Set Jack-o'-Lantern
To watch by the door.

To Bind Your Shadow

Close all windows,
Close all doors,
Utter not
A word aloud;
Cast the shadow
By a single
Candle, tall
And black as shade;
When the clock
Is striking twelve,
Take two lacquers,
Gold and silver;
Where your shape
Stands on the wall,
Paint with one
And then another;
Trace the edges
With your finger,
Quickly blow
The candle out—
Then though darkness
Fly from day
The midnight image
Has been caught.

For Ink from the Soft-Barked Sumac

For an ink to use in charmed inscriptions, take the Sumac's antlers crowned with leaves and fruit, boil them awhile in filtered rain, add a pinch of iron dust gathered with a magnet or lodestone, and then strain out the liquid, saying this:

Thicket secret,
Shallow, airy,
Horns of velvet,
Feathers many,
Green as water,
Red as flame—
Shed thy blood
And sign my name.

For Gathering Herbs on Midsummer's Eve

Go in moonlight
Or, if it be dark,
Take a lantern
With a white candle;
Stand where fern
Grows under the trees,
Listen until
The air is still;
Then you may speak:

On Midsummer's Eve
We hasten to weave
Fern and leaf
For every grief,
Stalk and seed
For every need.

Soon gather the fern
And fern seed; then
St. Johnswort, mullein,
Vervain, willow, elder,
Or what else you seek.

For Conjuring with Smoke

In an iron vessel burn
Mullein dried,
St. Johnswort fresh,
Willow old,
Wild lettuce green,
Apple dead,
Red cedar new:
While the living smoke ascends,
Let it wind about your hands
And shape it thus:

Breath and substance
Risen twice,
Death and issue,
Double face,
Phoenix fire,
Burning feather,
Fly and flower
All together.

Set it free and watch it rise:
Discover fate in this disguise.

For Seeing with Fire

No card or palm
Can tell you more
Than figures
In the winter fire;
Work the spell
Dried from leaves
Of crocus, rose,
Chrysanthemum;
Watch what form
Or sign may burn
Upon the air,
What face or name
Or number flares
Within the flame:

The spire of gold,
The willow green,
The silver snake,
The scarlet king,
The seven stars,
The broken chain,

May all be shown,
But if two hands
Wrought blue and thin

Be seen to rise
And curl and wring
Together, run
For water, quick—
Put out the blaze,
Then leave it dark
For seven days.

To Pass through a Locked Door

Where the lock
Is filled with rust
And all the keys
Have long been lost,
And time has warped
The heavy door
Against the place
It fit before,
And no one can
Remember now
What joys or sorrows
It could show,
Then you must tap
Its silent boards
Once, twice, and thrice,
And say these words:

Whatever lies
Beyond this door
Let me enter
Without fear,
Or else with lever,
Saw, and axe,
I'll serve the wood
Until it breaks.

If its panels
Do not fall,
Its frame unfasten
From the wall,
And show the hidden
Scene to you,
You are not worthy
Of the view.

To Weave Ropes of Sand

The devil spins
This task for us
That he may laugh—
But do it thus:
When first Sun
Shines on the sea,
Pick up a broken shell;
Smooth a space
Where the sands are firm,
And write these letters well:

```
    R
    O
ROPES
    E
    S
```

The words you weave
Will make him fly,
For crossed ropes
Must hang him high.

To See the Faces of Past and Present

Set on a table by candlelight these tokens: a cup, an egg, a knife, a red cloth, a white cloth, a green leaf, a brown nut, a crystal, and a key. Place in their center some fragment of a looking-glass; look on yourself therein and say:

> *In the mirror space,*
> *In the mirror time,*
> *In my eye the mirror*
> *Holding what is mine:*
> *In the cup, the key,*
> *In the sea, the knife,*
> *In the egg, the sun,*
> *In the nut, the leaf.*

Wrap the cup, the egg, the nut, and the looking glass in the cloth of white; wrap the knife, the leaf, the key, and the crystal in the cloth of red. Bury the first to the east of your house, and the second to the west. Thus live in peace between bodies remaining and energies acting, between instances reflecting and instants refracting.

To Seek That Which Has Been Lost

The smallest mote
Of dust mislaid
May be recovered
By this aid:
Place in an eggshell
All of these—

The pollen basket of a bee,
The golden eye-ring of a frog,
The unripe seeds of violets,
The pollen of a columbine,
One mushroom from a fairy-ring,
A strand of spider gossamer,
A drop of milk-white milkweed sap,
A single thread of thistledown.

Shake them gently,
Spill them out
Onto a folded
Colored cloth;
Their pattern then
Will tell the spot
Where you may seek
The missing thing—

Yet even though
You find it not,
You will have gathered
Treasures as fine
As any lost.

To Become the Likeness of a Bee

Pound in a mortar
A pint of purple
Clover flower,
Pour in honey
From half a comb;
Mix to an ointment,
Spread on the skin,
And repeat this charm:

Golden pollen,
Golden bee,
Let me shrink
As small as thee.

Wings clear as water
Will sprout
On your back,
A yellow velvet
Will fur you over,
And all the world
Grow high
About your head.

For Telling Fortunes by Sand

On a red paper
Spread dry sand;
Draw with the finger
A circle there;
Gather the grains
Outside the rim
And let them run
From the left palm, slowly
Down to the circle's
Center, saying:

Time is truth
Time is sand
Time run true
From my own hand:
For love
For joy
For pain
For death . . .

Repeat these four;
When the sand ends,
In that word
The truth will rest.

For Telling Fortunes by Tea Leaves

To see your future, dark or fair,
Conjure the leaves left in the cup:
Circle its handle three times round,
Turn it over and turn it up—
Read the pattern of joy and pain
Upon this map, from depth to rim:

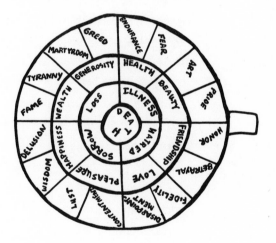

For Naming Familiars

Those pets who abide
And watch at your side,
Your cause to befriend,
Your will to attend,
Your arts to approve,
Your ills to remove,
Must serve and be mute—
But give them delight
By learning with care
The names that they bear:
Ninx is the fish
And *wix* is the bat,
Pibbit the mouse
And *leppin* the rat,
Lurit the finch,
Oxpictas the owl,
Scridee the sparrow,
Runipia the fowl,
Quist is the beetle
And *crope* is the mole,
Yim the opossum
And *sylog* the snail,
Jalp is the pig,
Pronocaspo the deer,

Ircis the otter,
Iltorep the bear,
Jubbin the toad
And *morling* the frog,
Ninkip the cat
And *malop* the dog,
Smeth is the fly
And *sordoxo* the stoat,
Galosty the lamb,
Hurathixet the goat.
Address them as these
If their ears you would please.

For an Astrology Amended and Reversed

Two faults the ancient zodiac bears:
One, that it lags behind the years,
The other, that when its stars mount high
Sun is there too, and blinds the eye;
Thus you must free the signs of fate
And set the wandering seasons straight:

The *Ram* that leapt over hills of spring
Must now run into the *Bull's* round ring,
And thence be led to the other side
Of the year, allowing the *Scales* to ride
That zone where the *Bull* so long has stood
But leaves, to bellow in autumn's wood;
Thus where the *Ram* has left his hills,
The *Fishes* would spawn in freshening rills,
But they must swim to the nether seas
And herald the frost in autumn skies;
Then who shall announce when spring has come?
The *Virgin*, high on her nightly throne
When Sun is hidden behind the world
And cannot enter her zenith cold;
She shall be followed by *Balances* fair,
Then *Scorpius* creeping along the air;
The *Archer's* bow shall learn to raise
Into the firmament summer's days;

Thereafter the *Goat* shall charge the night
When men grow fierce with lingering heat,
Until the *Water-Carrier* quench
This fever, and tip his jar to drench
The course where the *Fishes* attend their spawn,
And the *Ram* and the *Bull* shall follow soon;
The *Twins* mark winter, and in their wake
The *Crab* and the *Lion* their sequence take
In angry snow and winds as sharp
As claws, to finish the seasons' arc.

Then as in spring the *Virgin* rises,
Loosed from that earlier law's devices,
Know her reborn, and take her hand,
Follow her through the enlightened band
Where you may reign in the Sun's old place,
And read the universe face to face.

The Cosmos

For Reading a Sundial

Honor the Sun upon its way;
Stand by the dial at noon, and say:

I am thy Gnomon
And thy man:
I mark the circle
Of thy flame.

These are the words the dial's face
Should bear, to follow Sun's long pace:

MAN TO SUN I BIND:
EACH ALONE IS BLIND.

For Sunrise at the Summer Solstice

When June is ripe
And the days are full
And Sun comes early
To claim his throne,
Walk before dawn
To a silent height
And set three stones
In an eastward line;
Stand behind them
While his light
Is rising over
The distant land;
When he is there
In the eastern air,
Offer these words:

Sun of the year
I move this earth
To greet thy sign,
And set myself
To honor thee
In the earth's design.

Perfect the stones
To mark his face,
Follow their shadow
Twelve short paces,
Pluck some leaf
For an amulet.

To Enlist the Elements' Aid for a High Cause

Mark this figure on the ground,
In its quartered center stand,
Face the compassed circle round,
Saying this, the world to bind:

Sun of the east
And western sky,
Northern lode
That guards the pole,
Sea of the south,
My ancient blood,
Points and elements
Work my goal:
All that I ask
Is thy desire,
All that I seek

Is for thy care;
My earth is thine,
And thine my fire,
Our waters one,
My breath thy air.

Then name your favor—if it seem
An object worthy of this scheme.

To Conjure the Weather

Say this to greet
The morning sky
When early light
First meets your eye:

Sun, rain,
Cloud, snow,
I rise up
And over you go—
To bend
My way,
To serve
My day.

Then and later
Must all chill
Or fiery weather
Keep you well.

To Bring Rain

Set upon rocks an iron pot,
Kindle beneath it a fire hot,
Fill it half with water new,
Then add these, to build the brew:
An unbound rope,
A bar of soap,
A drop of oil,
A pinch of soil,
A buckthorn sprig,
A maple twig,
A broken bag,
A tattered rag,
A spoonful of salt,
A rusted bolt.
When these break to a boiling froth,
Brandish a hammer over the broth,
Strike it thrice on the vessel's side,
Calling these words to the weathers wide:

Hither, cloud,
And loose thy flood;
Wither, drought,
Let rain come out!

Sprinkle the potion over the grass—
That which you ask shall come to pass.

To Be Said in a Thunderstorm

Thunder my anger,
Lightning my might:
I take them in
I send them out
Over wind and night,
To serve me well
To save me well
To harm nothing under my sight.

To Stop Rain from Falling

If the rain has beaten down
Seven days without the sun,
While an ever-blowing wind
Bends the flowers to the ground,
And trodden grasses turn to mud,
The sodden gardens to a flood,
You must go and stand alone
On a height of barren stone;
Take with you an empty sack,
Hold it open, then, and speak:

Water, rain,
And flooded sky,
Let the weeping
Earth be dry;
Wind be silent,
Black cloud, break—
Now into my sack
For Earth's sweet sake!

Let it billow, full and wide,
Close it up with air inside;
Tie it tight with purple, red,
Green and blue and yellow thread;
Bury it in a garden bed—
The sun shall bloom, the storm lie dead.

For Reviving the Earth Spirit

When deadly frost has touched the ground,
And turned its fertile flesh to bone,
You may bring it to life again:
Break the soil and spade it fine,
Gather it, pot it, take it in
To soften by the fire's flame;
Anoint it with fresh water then,
Breathe its breath, and name its name:

Spirit of Earth
Arise and live:
I break the frost
And open thy grave.

To Honor a Tree at the Vernal Equinox

When nights and days
Are balanced and halved,
Cut from the branches
March has saved
Twelve supple wands,
All budded and green,
Twist them together
To weave a crown,
And say these lines:

Summer will come, and the autumn wind,
Turning and turning the leaves on their stems:
Then they must fall, but now in the spring
The twig is bound, and the bud remains.

Hang the wreath
From a sturdy limb
Of oak or maple,
Ash or elm;
Thus will the tree
Live well and long.

For Discovering Tree Spirits

When the Moon is round
In spring or summer,
Go to a place
Where more than two
But not over twenty
Trees are growing,
Measure their bounds
By silent walking,
Mark their center
And in it stand,
But make no sound;
Listen and watch
And you may find
Green and silver
Shadows flying
From leaf to leaf,
And a noise like water
Or quiet talking;
Strike three times
With a stick of oak
Upon the ground—
Then you may see
In every tree
The falling streams

Of their silver hair,
And their hands
Like silver-flickering air;
Their frightened emerald
Eyes will stare
Until you look away——
Then though you stay
For a year and a day,
You will not see them again.

Of Poisons to Beware

Take care that none of these,
Proud and precious
Though they be,
For magic and for ornament,
Shall touch your mouth:

The Christmas rose and mistletoe,
The leaves or twigs of cherry,
The rhubarb leaf, the sprig of yew,
The oak and elderberry,
Potato vine, potato sprout,
The privet and the laurel,
Narcissus, raw marsh-marigold,
Poppy and may-apple,
The monkshood, the foxglove,
The buttercup and daphne,
Corn cockle, cow cockle,
Snakeroot, pokeweed,
Moonseed, the hemlocks,
The nightshades, red or black,
Baneberry, larkspur,
Horsetail and bracken,
Henbane and dogbane
And false hellebore,
And even certain other names
Not named here—

For Earth has her mysteries,
And if you mock their wealth
She will offer you
A deep grave,
Garlanded with death.

To Atone for Cutting Down a Tree

Whether fear or foolish thought
Or mere necessity has brought
The haughty elm or poplar down,
For its expense you must atone:
Face the mourning field or wood
Or barren space where once it stood,
And offer penance to the tree,
Lest blight and sorrow fall on thee:

Poor spirit hurled
From proud estate,
I rue the deed
I did of late:
Forgive my axe
That thee did vex,
And spare my life
Thy grievous fate.

For Preserving the Sunflower

The Sun must lose his rays
When autumn bows him down,
Yet a hundred summer days
Fill the circle of his crown;
Hang his image up to dry
From a rafter dark and high,
Hold this promise to his eye:

From winter's greed
I'll save thy seed,
But when the snow
Is gone, I'll go
And sow it round
Within the ground
To raise thy gold
A hundredfold.

For Keeping Dried Grasses

When all the woods are dying,
And the mournful geese are flying
With a call like distant hounds
Past the gray horizon's bounds,
And forgotten apples freeze
On the ground beneath the trees,
And the butterflies, undone,
Turn despairing from the sun,
And the flowers fall and rust,
Curling to a sorry dust,
Still the seedy grasses stand—
Pale, where they were green and grand,
Yet like spears against the air,
Shaped as perfect as they were
Gather them if you would know
How to last the winter through;
Set them dry within a jar,
Honored as spring flowers are;
Keep them all the winter long;
Sing for them this human song:

Immortal grass,
Let winter pass
So neither leaf,
Nor seed, nor life,
Within this house
May come to grief.

To Dismiss Winter Greens

All trees or boughs
That have been cut
And kept for luck
Within the house
Must not be cast
Away and scorned,
But gravely burned
To dust at last;
Chop them fine,
Give them flame,
Offer this rhyme:

Forgive our fire,
Faithful tree:
Warm us now
Who have warmed thee.

To Say to a Fox

When fox-red suns
Burn low in the south,
The cold fox turns
To famine and death;
But leave by his house
Four rats, three birds,
Two hares and a mouse
And these warm words:

Fox run round
And favor my ground;
Eat from my hand,
Fatten my land

Who feeds a fox
Should suffer no loss.

To Converse with a Snake

Speak to the serpent
With his voice,
In the language
Of his race,
Slow and sliding,
Softly chiding,
Sweet and gliding,
Sly, confiding:

SITSIP
PTISLI
TSLSIL
TLISSA

Say it, gazing
In his eyes—
His subtle tongue
Will turn you wise.

For Hearing the Words of Mice

Enter a house
Where no one lives,
Where the key is lost
To the open door;
Go at night
When yellow leaves
Are heavy with rain
And a coming frost;
Take no light
But a tallow candle,
Sit in a corner
Where spiders crawl;
Smother the flame
With a shower of dust,
Listen and listen
Against the wall.
Then you may hear,
Close to your ear:

Gather seeds
And gather thistles,
Quick before
The north wind whistles,
Build the nests
And gnaw the tunnels,

Shred the papers,
Steal the flannels:
Bring them soon
And weave them warm,
Lest we taste
The bitter storm!

But if not this,
Or something like it,
You will know
That the mice
Have found you out—
Still leave them
A cloth and a crust
Before you go.

For Catching Frogs

Walk the edge
Of the water
Back and forth
Three times, then stop
And count to three;
Where the frog lies,
Gaze at him
Until he moves—
Then say to him,

Frog I see thee
Frog I hold thee
To my eye
And to my will.

Catch him quick
In a stout net,
For if you fail at first,
You will fail at last.

To Be Spoken into a Seashell

If the seashell speaks
To you,
Then you may whisper
In its ear:

The sea
Has brought thee
Safe to shore:
By earth
And water
May I, too,
Be spared.

But then you must
Guard it
Safe somewhere,
Forevermore.

For Flying South with Swallows

Wet-gray air from the hills
Will find the swallows gone.
If you would go with them,
Rise before the Sun
When the Corn Moon has waned;
Kneel in a mown field,
And write these words
On a yellow leaf
With an eagle's quill:

Swallow, I would fly
To the southern sea;
Swallow, give me wings
To follow thee.

Stand, then, and cast the leaf
Into the air above your head:
If it blow north you shall remain;
If it blow east you shall be kept;
If it blow west you shall be bound;
If it blow south you shall be borne away.

For Good Fortune in Winter

When the evening fire
Lies down tame,
Take twelve twigs
Of ash or rowan,
Tied in thread,
Yellow or red,
And cast them in,
Thinking in silence
Of what you wish, whether
Love or wealth
Or gentle weather;
Watch their flame,
Do not look away
Until it dies,
And you shall have your way.

Against the Moon's Last Quarter

The Waning Moon
Flies low and late
With tainted horn
And tarnished wit;
If you would shun
Its fevered state,
Go forth and spit
Upon a stone
And say these lines:

Die, old Moon,
And do it quick,
Lest I, like thee,
Grow weak and sick.

To Be Said in the Dark of the Moon

Though maiden and matron
And crone have passed,
And heavy night
Must reign at last,
Never allow
The Queen to lie
Quenched in her deadly
Slough of sky—
Summon her powers,
Utter her names,
And she will rise up
Again in flames:

DIANA
LUNA
LUCINA
LUMEN
LUMEN
LUMEN

To Change Pebbles into Jewels

For rubies and emeralds
To hold in handfuls,
Amethysts and sapphires
To scatter in the air,
Beryls and opals
To fill your pockets with,
Paths of diamonds
To walk on carelessly,
Gather pebbles as white as ivory:
Wash some in wintergreen,
Wash some in wine,
Wash some in iodine,
Wash some in vinegar,
Wash some in almond oil,
Wash some in milk,
Then clean them well with soap and water;
Dry them and keep them
Dark in a box
That is lined with silk,
In a thrice-locked room,
Until the earth is covered with snow:
When the winter Moon
Is rising full,
And the planet Venus

Lies white in the west,
Spread them glittering
Under the sky,
Steep them in snowlight,
Moonlight, starlight,
The whole night through;
Then, if they do not clear
And color as they should,
It is not the spell gone wrong
But your own flawed eye.

To Keep a Soap Bubble from Breaking

When you have made
The floating sphere,
The globe of rainbow—
Streaming air,
Transparent world,
Trembling planet,
Shuddering star,
Great as your head
But thin as a thread
That wind can tear
From the spider's web,
Do not despair—
Let this be said:

That which is whole
Cannot be torn,
That which is woven
Cannot be worn:
Shiver and burst
On the Moon's white horn,
But out of the sun
Be ever born.

Then turn away;
Follow it not
With an anxious eye—
Your words will hold it,
Though it may fall
In tears, like meteors,
From the sky.

For Possessing a Star

If you will have
Antares,
Scarlet sting of Scorpius,
Or count for wealth
Capella,
Gold-fleeced goat,
Or *Rigel*, fire
Of sapphire, pivot
To Orion's pace,
Or *Sirius* his dog,
As white as ice, yet
Flashing every color,
Then go and find
The light you seek
Mirrored in water;
Break the wet glass,
Pluck out the star
By its radiant hair—
But do not dare
To look upon its face,
Lest you go blind;
Dig a pit in earth
And cast it in;
Cover it; bear it
Only in your mind.

A Confession of Mortality To Say upon a Meteor's Falling

While I see thee cross the sky,
To wake and live and burn and die
All in a flash, eternity
Watches me fall as swift as thee.

To See the Future

When Venus stands the morning star or the evening
star, seek her as she rises or sets. Carry with you an
orb of crystal, large or small but free from flaw, and
raise it up to catch her image: when she lies at its
center, gaze there and invoke her thus:

Thou fire, no fire but the Sun's most silver mirror,
Thou star, no star but solid globe like this I bear,
Thou disk, thou crescent, neither crescent nor disk but
sphere, seeming clear as glass is clear,
Thou planet veiled, whose face is a bright cloud more
radiant for its obscurity,
Thou mystery, whose shadows hide beneath the guise
of light,
Thou world, whose lands remain unknown while thou
shinest most evident of all beyond this world:
Reveal now, reveal to me here, all that is obscure and
hidden under day's illusion;
Reveal to me the nature of all that thou seest, set so far
from earthly lands, above earthly sight:
Appear to me here in this crystal which is thy likeness,

Appear now in the guise of substance beyond this
day's knowledge:
Soften, flow, clarify, reform thyself as the vision which
thou hidest, which emanates from thee, which partakes
of thy perspective across darkness; tell and foretell all for
my enlightenment, as thou
art indeed prophetic of the morning and the evening;
Give me thy wisdom concerning all things that lie
before the earth upon its path;
Translate thyself to cloud within clarity, clarity
within cloud, and show me here all that thou seest
and containest.

Study your globe in patience, then, for as long as the
planet's light remains undimmed; the knowledge you
seek shall be made manifest.

For Reconciliation with the Universe

In the dark of the Moon when stars show clear,
Go where no houses or lights appear,
Where hills are low and grass grows high;
Lie on your back beneath the sky,
Fix with your gaze the brightest star,
Speak this aloud, to answer its fire:

Lower than grass
My light began,
Into the heavens
Soon it ran:
Here between Earth
And space I shine,
My fallen dust
The twin to thine—
Star that I was,
Star that I am,
Star I shall be
My name is human.

Stand then, and tread the living air,
Ascend the vision's open stair;
Passing the planets' silent race,
Rise and mirror the cosmic face—
Infant of galaxies, prodigal Sun,
Resume this title: All and One.